BEST AFRICAN AMERICAN POEMS

Past and Present

Selected and Introduced by

W. Maurice Shipley, Ph.D.

and

Selected and Commentary by

Leonard A. Slade, Jr., Ph.D.

BEST AFRICAN AMERICAN POEMS

Past and Present

Selected and Introduced by

W. Maurice Shipley, Ph.D.

and

Selected and Commentary by

Leonard A. Slade, Jr., Ph.D.

XULON PRESS

Xulon Press
2301 Lucien Way #415
Maitland, FL 32751
407.339.4217
www.xulonpress.com

Paperback ISBN-13: 978-1-66287-987-6
Ebook ISBN-13: 978-1-66287-988-3

Contents

Introduction

<u>Early Poetry from Slavery to Freedom</u> (1770-1865)

"It is important that every people should have its own poetry, not simply for those who enjoy poetry-—such people could always learn other languages and enjoy their poetry but because it actually makes a difference to the society as a whole."

(T.S. Eliot)

The ethos of which African American poetry evolved is unique to African Americans. It is fraught with pain and suffering a-by-product of slavery and inhumanity. At the same time, African American poetry evolved in such a way as to motivate Black poets to move beyond racial barriers in order to reflect poetic traditions, techniques, and a sense of the poetic self-—engaging humanity.

History points to and notes the earlier poetry of poets such as Lucy Terry and Jupiter Hammon, but it does not necessarily underscore the importance of slave songs, ballads, chants and secular music-—as significant forerunners of African American poetry. To be sure, while poetry has strict forms and parameters, it lends itself much more to experimentalism, stylistics, subject examination, language, and purposes than any other form of writing.

With a nod to the earliest efforts of Lucy Terry ("Bars Fight") and Jupiter Hammon ("An Evening Thought: Salvation by Christ with Penitential Cries"), the earliest published poetry by an African American was written by Phyllis Wheatley, a very skilled poet, at the age of fourteen. Wheatley was essentially a poet looking for a sense of self, and finding her poetic voice-—one that might be accepted in a society that rejected all things Black.

Wheatley was an essentially "raceless" poet, yet her poetry had informative value. And, while she was an African born slave woman,

Wheatley was fortunate to acquire enough of an education as to become learned enough to write excellent elegiac verse. Her poem: "On the Death of the Rev. Mr. George Whitfield" (1770), is an excellent example of the elegiac format.

Wheatley has been criticized for the lack of any real sense of racial pride in her poetry. But such criticism is extremely short-sighted and totally ignores historical context. Most of Wheatley's poems pay homage to the Neoclassical tradition and point to a fairly imitative style. But one cannot ignore the human pain of loss in her poem: "On Being Brought from Africa to America" (1773). This is to suggest that Wheatley felt much more than she expressed in her poetry.

Wheatley's poetry set a "standard" for the early poetry of African American poets. Largely utilizing religion-—hymns and sermons, it tended to be impersonal, appealing to a sympathetic audience-—one that would understand the psychological and emotional ramifications of slavery. Her poetry helped to set the stage for poets such as George Moses Horton and Frances Watkins Harper. Indeed, their poetry is better understood in the context of African American poetry during the abolition movement and Reconstruction.

Slavery and Abolition (1800-1865)

The nineteenth century witnessed a whole new movement in African American poetry. The "pall" that had settled over the country, relative to Black activism focusing on the institution of slavery.

Former slave, George Moses Horton wrote such poems as, "The Slave's Complaint" (1829) and "Slavery." The poems demonstrate use of rhyming couplets that contain a rather narrow focus on the psycho-logical pain of slavery. Horton's poetry lacked the more sophisticated use of imagery and psychologically probing techniques of Frances Watkins Harper, who wrote such poems as: "The Slave Mother," and "Bury Me in a Free Land." Harper's poetry was very popular, partly because of its relative imitation of John Whittier, a Quaker poet, who wrote abolition poetry that was more concerned with its focus on inflated imagery or pathos. It was committed to didacticism, which undermined overall intent and purpose. Finally, Harper's poetry was important to the abolitionist movement, because it did a good job of illustrating the abuse inherent in slavery.

<u>Reconstruction</u> (1865-1915)

Without question, the best African American poet, during the Reconstruction, was Paul Laurence Dunbar, whose name is synonymous with the best dialect verse ever written. With his book, <u>The Lyrics of a Lowly Life</u> (1896), Dunbar set the stage for African American poets to utilize Black culture as a rich subject for their poetry. His poem, "We Wear the Mask," remains one of the best poems to ever take on the subject of Black minstrelsy and the heartfelt pain of those, who felt "forced" to either be that which they were not or those who felt "forced" to accept that which was painful while they smiled-—pretending not to be affected by the pain.

Fenton Johnson is noteworthy for his poetic contributions during Reconstruction. He began writing poetry at an early age. By the time he began college, Johnson began to look at the works of accomplished poets such as Carl Sandberg, an early influence on Johnson-—especially Sandberg's focus on urban life. Johnson interwove his focus on rural Blacks with Sandberg's focus on the urban South in order to write about how urban life failed to support the souls of Black people, who were far closer to the rural life ("Tired") that comes with a pretending face.

Paul Laurence Dunbar was the first Black poet to achieve national recognition, primarily because his poetry was very poignant in the way it captured the plight of Black people, as well as the humor, pathos and aspirations of a suffering people. Known primarily as a folk poet, Dunbar utilized dialect verse to capture the realistic nuances of Black life. The unique poetic aspect of dialect infused Dunbar's characters with the myriad qualities of Black culture that streamlined poetic language was unable to achieve. The ability to "feel" a specific character enhanced reader enjoyment and enabled empathy for a marginalized culture.

Dunbar's poetry was enjoyed and praised in many circles. Unfortunately, much of the praise he received was largely for the wrong person. He noted that reason in both "The Poet," and "Compensation." He was specific in "The Poet," where he wrote: "But alas! the world came to praise a jungle in a broken tongue." The public that praised his poetry for the realism of the spoken word, but took their enjoyment as "fun" of a culture that was desperately seeking legitimacy and appreciation.

The Harlen Renaissance (1915-1930)

The development of African American poetry had a seamless transition between the Reconstruction poetry of Paul Laurence Dunbar and the Harlem Renaissance poetry of Langston Hughes. The most notable difference is the vision that Hughes consciously saw himself as a part of a literary movement and its importance in the development of African American people in America. One need only to read what Hughes wrote in his essay: "The Negro Artist and the Racial Mountain," where Hughes wrote:

> "We younger Negro artists who create now intend to
> express our individual dark-skinned selves without fear
> or shame. If white people are pleased, we are glad. If
> they are not, it doesn't matter. We know that we are
> beautiful and ugly too. The tom-tom cries and the
> tom-tom laughs. If colored people are pleased, we are
> glad. If they are not, their displeasure doesn't matter
> either. We build our temples for tomorrow strong as

we know how and we stand on top of the mountain free within ourselves."

The Harlem Renaissance was both a cultural and racial awakening for Black writers, the effects of which were felt by Blacks throughout the country. Blacks felt a sense of pride in who they were and began to see themselves as a viable part of America-—an important part of its cultural fabric. Langston Hughes, who came to be referred to as "The Poet Laureate of Harlem," was largely seen in a leadership role, along with W.E.B. DuBois and Alain Locke. Poetry was integral to the growth of the movement. The poetry of Langston Hughes, Countee Cullen, Claude McKay and Jean Toomer was considered some of the best poetry ever written by Black poets-—at that point in time.

Sterling Brown is rarely studied, in the context of the Harlem Renaissance, largely because of his exceptional literary criticism. But Brown was also a gifted poet. One need only to read his poem, "Strong Men," which serves to note the steady movement of a culture-—forward, and growing stronger, because the movement is that which is historically undergirded.

The poets of the Harlem Renaissance were determined to express the hopes, dreams, pain, sorrow, of a people desperately trying to be recognized as part of a country which failed to acknowledge either their contributions or very existence.

The poetry of Claude McKay is generally perceived to be volatile, because McKay was an angry man. McKay began writing dialect verse in the West Indies while searching for a form that would enable him to write the kind of poetry he most desired to write. Early on, McKay chose his rhymes and melodies by instinct. Ultimately, he came to focus on the poetic sonnet. That is where McKay's best poems are realized. The sonnet form demands a strong sense of control. Hence, McKay's anger is contained, and his poems illustrate a vision rich in its imagery and perceptions. "The White House," and "The Harlem Dancer," are excellent examples of his use of the sonnet form and are poignant examples of the excellence that is derived when subject is interwoven with vision, and poetic structure. McKay might have become a more accomplished poet had he been able to reconcile his conflicting feelings between Jamaican Island culture and an urban metropolis. That conflict made him feel like an "outsider."

McKay's feelings of being an "outsider" are not too unlike Countee Cullen's and his development as a poet. When Countee Cullen came to the Renaissance, he was a brilliant college educated poet, who had studied the great poets of the world. He was steeped in knowledge about poetic traditions. Unfortunately, Cullen's upbringing conflicted with his poetic development. Deeply, influenced by his adoptive father, who was a church minister, Cullen often found his poetic vision in conflict with his religious upbringing. His early poems, such as "The Black Christ" and "Yet I do Marvel" are excellent examples of Cullen's use of religion interwoven into his poetic vision.

Cullen had studied the great poets and developed a certain reverence for poetry. Such is evidenced in his early observation mirroring Samuel Coleridge that poetry had to have "lofty thoughts beautifully expressed." And, while he was often conflicted between religion and cultural expression, Cullen was often at his best when he wrote verse imitating the poet he most revered and often dedicated various poems to him-—Romantic poet, John Keats.

Black Arts Movement (1960-1970)

The 1960's represented a volatile period in both the country in general and Black culture specifically. A new generation of African American emerged from colleges across the nation. Many were not predisposed to following the footsteps of parents and various Black artists, led by Amiri Baraka (aka LeRoi Jones), became more race-focused.

Baraka, a well-educated, brilliant writer left academia to become a leader of a movement termed: "The Black Arts Movement." Under his leadership, Black poets altered their poetic vision to embrace one which was race driven. He advocated a commitment to write poetry that focused on "liberating" Black people. Poets such as Sonia Sanchez, Nikki Giovanni, Haki Madhubuti (aka Don Lee), Mari Evans, and Dudley Randall (among others) embraced a poetic vision committed to what became known as "functional art" (i.e., poetry that was instructional insofar as "liberating" Black people-—a move from a sense of passivity to that which advocated taking control of one's destiny).

Baraka's poem, "Black Art," not only set the stage for a period in which Black American poetry focused on the didactic, but stated that: "Poems are bullshit, unless they are/teeth or trees or lemons piled/on a step. . .."/ "We want poems/like fists. . .." Such poems utilized a concept referred to as "Art as a weapon," which was utilizing language that functioned to inform the readers about how to respond to an aggrieved situation. Poets such as Sonia Sanchez, Nikki Giovanni, Haki Madhubuti, Mari Evans, Dudley Randall, among others, embraced a poetic vision committed to what was really "didactic poetry." In other words, "functional art" made little allowances for expanding and expressing poetry that was born of creative vision.

In important ways the "Black Arts Movement" had a dramatic impact on the kinds of poetry that dominated the decade of the 60's, but it did not stop many African American poets from writing great poetry. Indeed, great poetry will always stand the test of time.

<u>Modernism and Beyond</u> (Since 1970)

When one looks at the development of African American poetry in the context of modernism and understanding where African American poets are today, it isn't difficult to both see and understand. The current generation of African American poets did not just arrive on the literary scene. Many contemporary poets are steeped in academic studies-—studying a myriad great poet, of all cultures. They are not studying to imitate others. Rather they are seeking excellence-—first, by studying excellence. Further, they are studying the many poetic techniques, in order to find that which best conveys their vision. They are spending time learning relevant histories and cultures. Finally, both younger and older have come to understand that if a poet wishes to write poetry that speaks to hopes, dreams, and realities of any people he/she must know and understand the cultural needs of those people.

Three poets, who have come to be recognized for their poetry since 1970 are Rita Dove, Maya Angelou and Leonard A. Slade, Jr. Each has been widely recognized and praised for their poetry, especially the breath of their poetry.

One of Angelou's earliest poems suggests that she had a certain reverence for Paul Laurence Dunbar's poem: "Sympathy." And while Angelou demonstrated her talent in her first book, <u>I Know Why the Caged Bird Sings</u>, she clearly had a poet's heart and vision when it came to understanding the "American experience" for Black people. Her poem, "Still I Rise," is a part of the poetic legacy that embraced the indomitable spirit of Black people in America-—to keep getting up and refusing to be defeated. She once noted that her poetry was also focused on a love for others and a need for individuals to make love of others more important in their lives. Much of Angelou's poetry lends itself to music and recitation. Indeed, Angelou was always a great reader of her poetry, perhaps because she was a performer early in her career. Her career was highlighted on the day she read her specially crafted poem "On the Pulse of Morning" at the inauguration of William J. Clinton's swearing in as the forty-second President of the United States.

Rita Dove and Leonard A. Slade, Jr. are very similar in many ways. Both have been writing close to the same period of time and both have been widely read and praised for their poetry.

Dove stated early in her poetic career, "As an artist, I shun political considerations and racial or gender partiality. . .." Dove was not turning away from her culture. That is obvious. She was seeking to have her poetry read and studied for what each poem said, at a moment in time-— an observation borne of a poetic vision. That is not unlike Langston

Hughes when he stated that he "did not wish to be perceived as a Negro Poet." Hughes did not want his poetry to be read and studied in a narrow, race restricted way. Both Dove and Hughes wanted the world to consider their poetry as part of the world's poetry. Dove brought to her poetry, a rigid and disciplined poetic eye.

Dove's poetry is extra ordinary in its use of rich imagery and characterization, but she is at her best when she focuses on the personal, whimsy, utilizing the autobiographical to shape a lyrical vision of her history. This is especially well captured in "The Yellow House" and "My Father's Telescope." Dove's poetic vision is especially poignant when she looks beyond cultures and focuses on the dilemmas of individuals. Her poem, "The Oriental Ballerina," beautifully tracks the dancer's beauty against the dream and its realities. And while Dove has a rather wide-angled poetic eye, one which does not immerse itself in race, she does not necessarily shy away from racial subjects. Her poem, dedicated to David Oalker, is an excellent example of the poet agonizing about the life a Black committed abolitionist and the tragedy of his life.

Dove is one of the more decorated African American poets in history. She became only the second Black woman poet to be awarded the U. S. Pulitzer Prize for Poetry in (1987) and, in 1993 became the first Black woman to be elected to serve as Poet Laureate in the United States. Dove published her first book of poetry (<u>The Yellow House on the Corner</u>), in 1980. She was praised by critics for her use of history and her lyrical style. Dove utilized her personal history to write poetry that was very revealing in its focus, on the lives of Black people.

In 1988, Leonard A. Slade, Jr. published the first of his more than twenty books of poetry. The title of his first collection is very interesting-— <u>Another Black Voice, A Different Drummer</u>. The title is noteworthy because it spans the whole of African American poetry which makes a very important "statement." One need only look as far back as poets like Langston Hughes or Rita Dove to see how those poets wished to be perceived for their poetic vision and the uniqueness of their poetry rather than a more racialized perception. At the same time, both poets take pride in the richness of their heritage.

Slade's collection notes that he is "A Different Drummer." The point is that his poetry was different-—it was the product of a different poet-—one who had studied and learned differently. Slade's poetry was a clarion call for readers to best understand his poetic vision was to note that his poetry, while part of a (long) tradition, was the product of his own unique way of writing out of that tradition. And he could not have been more astute in his perception.

During the period termed The Modernist Period, many African American poets have been part of the academic community. They have studied the craft as students, read the works of great poets, and taught students in academia. Those poets have taken time to find the best technique. Whether it is the use of rhyme, form, structure, etc., or the use of imagery, symbolism, language, etc., African American poets have really studied their craft before concretizing a poetic vision. We see this when we look at poets such as Countee Cullen, Langston Hughes, Robert Hayden, Audre Lorde, Nikki Giovanni, Sonia Sanchez, Amiri Baraka, Maya Angelou, Rita Dove, and Leonard A. Slade, Jr.

One can readily note the influences of Langston Hughes, Robert Frost, Paul Laurence Dunbar, and Walt Whitman in Slade's poetry. It is evidenced in Frost's sense of the descriptive and imagery of everyday life. It is in the jaunty rhythm in the poetry of Dunbar and romanticism of John Keats. Slade pays homage to those great poets/writers in his poem: "Whisper," when he writes:

"My day begins and ends
with whispers from masters
of the craft of writing"

More than any single poet, Slade's poetry is much more diversified in both its vision and subject matter. Notable in <u>Another Black Voice,</u>

<u>A Different Drummer</u> are: "Poem to an Apostle of Peace" and "I've Known Rivers" (A tribute to Langston Hughes).

When Slade comes to <u>Sweet Solitude</u> (2010), he speaks as the poet, whose senses are acute and in harmony with the world around him, as well as a memory that reveres the joy that it gives to the heart.

Slade's poem: "I Am a Black Man" is reminiscent of Mari Evans, <u>I am a Black Woman</u>-—a title in verse-—one that notes the kinship of history and memory.

Slade's poetry ranges from the sermon of a Southern preacher, to the beauty of a world that seems to go unnoticed, to the love of those around him-—his efforts to share an innate sense of love for all human kind.

Perhaps what sets Slade apart from so many other poets is his absolute fidelity to language, and its ultimate value to great poetry. His concern for and use of language mirrors that which great poets of the past have espoused, such as T.S. Eliot, Samuel Coleridge, and William Wordsworth. In the words of W.H. Auden: "A poet is before anything else, a person who is passionately in love with language." "Coleridge wrote: "Poetry is the best words in their best order," finally, it is T.S. Eliot who, perhaps said it best, when he said: "We may say that the duty of the poet, as poet, is only indirectly to his people: his direct duty is to his language, first to preserve, and second to extend and improve."

Slade focuses on the importance of language both within his poems as well as by subject. One need only read his poem: "The Problem," in order to best understand that Slade is a poetry technician. And that's why he has been the recipient of numerous awards for his many books of poetry.

Slade's poetry has been roundly praised by poets such as Gwendolyn Brooks, Maya Angelou, and Nikki Giovanni. His poetry is a testimony to a poet, who richly deserves his place among the best poetic voices in African American poetry.

W. Maurice Shipley, Ph.D.
Formerly, The Ohio State University

Evangelist of Verse

Leonard A. Slade, Jr. preaches the gospel of poetry. A chat with him is a conversation brimming with verse – with recitations and panegyrics on the beauty, the nature the importance of the literary arts. He utters his favorite poems with fervidness and love, quoting them like scripture. He speaks of poetry as a light in the darkness, a solace in a broken world and a "tonic for the soul."

"The world is a better place – becomes a better place – when people read poetry," says the poet and longtime professor at the University at Albany, tucked into his favorite booth at Red Lobster on Wolf Road.

Slade is savoring the tilapia while talking about poetry. April is National Poetry Month, a designation he's celebrating with an April 14 event high lighting his latest published collections: "Poems for People of All Ages" and "I, Too, Am America." Everyone, he says, should take the time "to study poetry, to read poetry, to celebrate poetry in our schools and at our colleges and universities and synagogues and churches."

But not just in April. Every month is poetry month for a man who practices the art, sings its power and evangelizes its virtues with zeal. "There's a need for me, as a poet, to address the timeless hunger of the human spirit. ... Considering the problems that we're having in our world – not just in our country, but in other countries in the world today – if you ask me, we need poetry and art now more than ever. And to celebrate it! And share it!"

Gwendolyn Brooks defined poetry as "the distillation of the human experience." It's about life distilled," Slade says. "It's about life, the problems of this world, the joys, sorrows, beauty, ugliness, good, evil – evaluated, written about. So people need to have that level of consciousness heightened. Poetry does that. It feeds the soul."

Or, to cite another of his favorites: " 'Poetry is the rhythmical creation of beauty' whose purpose is to 'elevate the soul.' " That's Edgar

Allan Poe. Slade loves that definition, and he loves Poe, for reasons not wholly related to soul elevation, more on that later. The 19th-century American literary giant is among the many he quotes in his introduction to "I, Too, Am America," the title itself a reference to a Langston Hughes poem that Slade recites over lunch:

I am the darker brother.
They send me to eat in the kitchen
When company comes…
They'll see how beautiful I am
And be ashamed-
I, too, am America."

Slade's own poems are rich with history and image but clear-eyed, accessible, direct. He cites as influences some of his early teachers at summer writers' workshops in the 1980's, among them Stephen Dunn at Bennington and Donald Justice at Middlebury College. "I love their poetry," he says. "I'm still trying to emulate them."

Since then, he's earned multiple accolades for his verse, including, in 2015, a national poetry prize being named in his honor by the Southern Conference on African American Studies. The two new collections make 21 books of poetry Slade has published over the years, complementing an academic career that includes scholarly analyses of symbolism in "Moby Dick" and biblical allusions in "The Grapes of Wrath." His students come first, he says. Teaching, grading, being available during office hours – all of that is his top priority. Writing comes second.

Still, it consumes him. Sometimes he writes poems at Red Lobster. Often he writes poems at church, arriving an hour early for 10 a.m. services at the Cathedral of All Saints in Albany. "Guess what I'm doing," he says, "I don't even meditate. I have my notebook with me. I'm writing poetry."

One recent Sunday, in the midst of March Madness, he wrote a poem about Sister Jean, the Loyola basketball chaplain who became a national sweetheart. He sent it off to her – no word back just yet. "It's one of my *at least* C/C-plus poems!" Slade declares, laughing. "It's one of my better poems, I love that poem."

As a boy growing up in North Carolina, he memorized poetry. As a young man, he quoted it cold. He still does, reciting Poe's "To Helen" with a fine and theatrical relish:

Helen, thy beauty is to me
Like those Nicéan barks of yore
That gently, o'er a perfumed sea,
The weary, way-worn wanderer bore
To his own native shore.

"When I was courting young ladies, I would recite that poem to some of them," he says. "They looked at me as though they thought I was crazy."

One didn't: his future wife, Roberta Hall, a musicologist who's taught at UAlbany, Siena, and Skidmore. "Oh she *loved* it," he confirms. This August they'll be celebrating their 50th anniversary. "I think we were destined to be together…If it had not been for my wife, I'm not sure that I would be a poet," he says.

She's the one who needled Slade into trying his hand – seriously – at poetry. It was 1985. He was "39-plus," a dean at Kentucky State University, and she was in the thick of graduate studies at the University of Chicago. After attending various literary events there, she informed her husband that he could write just as well as some of the poets she'd heard.

So he started writing poems. He started submitting them to journals. They started getting accepted. Soon he had 40 or 50, enough for a book: "Another Black Voice: A Different Drummer," published in 1988, the same year he arrived at UAlbany. "The rest is history," he says. To this day, Roberta Hall Slade is his toughest critic. "If it's not a good poem, guess what, she will say: "You may want to put that one in the trash and start over."

A longtime mentor – George Hendrick, now based at SUNY Stony Brook – gave Slade the idea for both new books, he says. He got to work on them in 2016: first came "Poems for People of All Ages," a cross-hatch of human experience outlined in 71 poems; then came "I, Too, Am America," 84 portraits from African-American history that starts with an 18th-century poet Phyllis Wheatley and concludes with Barack Obama:

> *We seek rights ancestors died for.*
> *We see Paradise here: flowers, sunlight,*
> *Clouds, the rain for growth and harvest*
> *In this new century of all colors.*

"This is my calling," Slade says, and indeed he means that in a religious sense. "This is a gift that God has given me that he wants me to use – he wants me to use my gift to help make not my world, not your world, but *his* world a better place."

—Amy Biancolli
Reprinted by permission of the <u>Times Union</u>

They Will Be Gone Forever

By Leonard A. Slade, Jr.

"And the world passeth away…but he that doth the will of God
abideth forever."
John 2: 16, 17

They attacked the people's house
Because their national leader
Told them to do so.
He would march with them he said.
Their loyalty was 77% approval rating
Of their god who had lost a presidential election.
No tear gassing like the Black Lives Matter Protest.
Permission given by some Capitol police
To use rubber bullets and baton
They broke windows
Destroyed doors
Destroyed furniture
Ransacked offices
In a nation's Capitol
Citadel of America's democracy.
I see them obey a delusional psychopath
Desecrating the people's house
Trespassing vandalizing reclaiming
Power they lost during the presidential election
Determined to follow their
King of the universe who could
Not accept reality about himself and his world
The pandemic ignored
Consequences would come
Prison sentences impeachment

Deaths in the people's house
In nursing homes and hospitals.
What would it all mean?
With democracy under assault
Hearts broken in a political swamp
The nuclear button would not be touched
Souls would be transformed
Civilization would be saved
Problems for the new leader would be solved
During the Existential crisis
Faith hope and charity
Would save a country
That would take its citizens to a hill
And watch stars and the moon
Believers who would step out of the darkness
Where a cult leader
A sick unstable puppy
Left the White House
Ashamed humiliated evil
Returning eventually to the bowels of the earth
Where worms would suck his eyes
And savor his balls as an appetizer
His heart eaten and bones sucked
The people's house remains standing
For thousands of years to come.

6 January 2021

Best African American Poems

Past and Present

1. Lucy Terry ("Bars Fight")
2. Phillis Wheatley ("To His Excellency General Washington," "On Being Brought From Africa to America," "On Virtue"
3. Jupiter Hammon
   "An Evening Thought: Salvation by Christ"
4. George Moses Horton
   "The Slave's Complaint"
   "The Art of a Poet"
   "Slavery"
   "A Lover's Farewell"
5. Paul Laurence Dunbar
   "We Wear the Mask"
   "Sympathy"
   "The Poet"
   "When Malindy Sings"
6. Alice Dunbar Nelson
   "I Sit and Sew"
   "April Is On The Way"
7. Angelina Grimke
   "A Mona Lisa"
   "Grass Fingers"
   "The Black Finger"
8. Fenton Johnson
   "Tired"
   "The Lonely Mother"
   "The Old Repair Man"
9. Gwendolyn Brooks
   "The Mother"
   "Mentors"
   "We Real Cool"

62. Julia Fields
    "High on the Hog"

Afterword

African American poetry "has been the essence of a people's culture, saying who they are, the ways they feel, the ways they interact with and view the world," observed Mari Evans. Poetry helps us to define ourselves. After all, it has "a music of its own, a music everyone can hear, regardless of the instrumentation," Evans opines.

Edgar Allan Poe states, "Poetry is the rhythmical creation of beauty whose purpose is to elevate the souls." Gwendolyn Brooks states, "Poetry is the distillation of human experience, of life distilled." African American poets write poetry that delights the ear, appeals to our imagination, and calms the agitation of the soul. Good poetry is an artistic expression of significant ideas written to delight the ear and feed the soul. African American poets have mastered stylistic devices and choice of words. They have also touched our emotions, shared truth, and made harmonious music. Langston Hughes once wondered who would write more African American poems. He stated with pride, "It'll be me, myself, yes, it'll be me." Indeed, as Evans observes, we find "energy, excitement, and substance in Black poetry." The best African American poems continue to be written with clarity, erudition, style, and grace.

Finally, this poet believes, the best African American poems contribute to the intellectual and aesthetic enlargement of lives and help the human spirit triumph in our complex world. Let it be said a thousand years from now that poetry helped to save our world and that the power and beauty of our best poets' works contributed to the survival of civilization.

—Leonard A. Slade, Jr., Ph.D.
Formerly, State University of New York at Albany

After the Slap

By Leonard A. Slade, Jr.

Whoever slapped hard would suffer something
that was on stage
millions worldwide watching.

The walk would be devilish, a pow
on a jaw. He'd shock
the victim into grace,

he'd evoke silence, anything
for some redemption. They'd wait
for the Best Actor announcement.

The wife was to admire as if he hadn't
wronged, a gesture
so belligerent

it would destroy the joke,
or the curse while protecting
a sweetheart

of clean hair, mahogany beauty
admired by spectators. They couldn't
two brothers

each globalizing hatred one night.
Each knew better, each knew
the other's weakness

Would create weaponed laughter, the silence hoped
for the forgiveness undeserved
of breath and expletives.

Why? Where? It was Oscar night, always
At its best performance, but
Maybe next time.

This celebration

there were tears from the best actor;
his hurt wife basking in the glory
to say her husband loved her

to pieces. And their celebration would
suffer the consequences, a slap
burning with regret.

—Leonard A. Slade, Jr.
The Boulé Journal
Printed by permission

Acknowledgments

The editors thank Ms. Sue Shipley, Ms. Roberta Hall Slade, Mr. Paul Grondahl, Mr. Gary Hahn, Ms. Marcy Casavant, Mr. Kephra Burns, President Havidan Rodriguez, Beta Psi Boulé of Sigma Pi Phi Fraternity, The Times Union, President Raymond M. Burse, The Ohio State University, and the State University of New York at Albany for their ardent support of this publication.

References

African American Literature: Voices in Tradition
    Holt, Rinehart and Winston, 1992

The Oxford Anthology of African American Poetry
    Edited by Arnold Rempersad
    Oxford University Press, 2006

The Boule Journal
    Sigma Pi Phi Fraternity
    Volume 86 / Number 82 / Summer 2022

Responding to the Poems
By Leonard A. Slade, Jr.

1. How do individual poems provide understandings of the past or present? Which poems?

2. What are the multiple possible meanings of several of your favorite poems? Do they undermine traditional interpretations?

3. What is the central theme of ten poems in the book?

4. How do parts of the poem relate to the theme?

5. What are six figures of speech used in six poems which objectify the meanings of the works?

6. What are a few concrete images in your favorite poems that create mental pictures for you?

7. What is the tone of a few poems written in the 19th Century? Compare and contrast the tone with a few more contemporary African American poems.

8. Comment on the rhythm of (beat, meter) Langston Hughes' poems. Compare his rhythm with another poet's rhythm.

9. How do some poems portray men and women?

10. How do some of the best poems portray upper or lower classes? Compare and contrast six poems.

11. How do poets treat the subject of love? Hatred? Racism? Sexism?

12. What are some allusions in poems that are most striking?

13. Which poems use Biblical allusions as a frame of reference?

14. Which poems use the strongest verbs that are precise and powerful?

15. Which poems are written in free verse (without stanza form, rhyme scheme, or meter)?

16. Which lyric poems express personal thoughts and feelings?

17. Which poems use black music as a frame of reference?

18. Which poems use the historic past as a frame of reference?

19. Which poems are the strongest religious poems? Explain.

20. Which poems are the best love poems? Explain.

21. Which poems are the strongest social protest poems?

22. Which poems are the best examples of the Italian, or Petrarchan sonnet made up of two parts: an octave (eight lines) and a sestet (six lines)? Explain.

23. Which poems have the best examples of alliteration? Explain.

24. Which six poems affect you? Explain.

25. Which poems make you think of your ancestors? Explain.

26. Which poems use plain speech to convey meanings?

27. Do you know the meanings of all the words in your favorite poems? Which poems are the most philosophical? Esoteric?

28. Examine the structure of some of the best poems.

29. Which poems are the most powerful?

30. Which poems made you cry? Explain.

31. Which poems made you happy? Explain.

32. What is your overall evaluation of Best African American Poems: Past and Present?

W. Maurice Shipley is Professor Emeritus at the Ohio State University, where he taught African American Literature and many other courses. He was the recipient of the Excellence in Teaching Award, among others, and has read papers at national professional meetings. He has also published articles in national learned  journals. He earned the Ph.D. degree in English from the University of Illinois at Urbana-Champaign, where he studied with Nina Baym, Distinguished Professor of English and American Literature. Dr. Shipley has hosted The College Language Association Convention at The Ohio State University and has shared his brilliant literary criticism at U.S. Colleges and Universities. He has taught at Wabash College (Indiana) and at Temple University. His duties as a chief administrator at The Ohio State University were rooted in his pure literary scholarship, for which he has received national notoriety.